AF007062

Dick Whittington

A Pantomime

Verne Morgan

A Samuel French Acting Edition

FOUNDED 1830

SAMUELFRENCH-LONDON.CO.UK
SAMUELFRENCH.COM

Copyright © 1982 by Verne Morgan
All Rights Reserved

DICK WHITTINGTON is fully protected under the copyright laws of the British Commonwealth, including Canada, the United States of America, and all other countries of the Copyright Union. All rights, including professional and amateur stage productions, recitation, lecturing, public reading, motion picture, radio broadcasting, television and the rights of translation into foreign languages are strictly reserved.

ISBN 978-0-573-16422-4

www.samuelfrench-london.co.uk

www.samuelfrench.com

FOR AMATEUR PRODUCTION ENQUIRIES

UNITED KINGDOM AND WORLD EXCLUDING NORTH AMERICA
plays@SamuelFrench-London.co.uk
020 7255 4302/01

Each title is subject to availability from Samuel French, depending upon country of performance.

CAUTION: Professional and amateur producers are hereby warned that *DICK WHITTINGTON* is subject to a licensing fee. Publication of this play does not imply availability for performance. Both amateurs and professionals considering a production are strongly advised to apply to the appropriate agent before starting rehearsals, advertising, or booking a theatre. A licensing fee must be paid whether the title is presented for charity or gain and whether or not admission is charged.

The professional rights in this play are controlled by Samuel French Ltd, 52 Fitzroy Street, London, W1T 5JR.

No one shall make any changes in this title for the purpose of production. No part of this book may be reproduced, stored in a retrieval system, or transmitted in any form, by any means, now known or yet to be invented, including mechanical, electronic, photocopying, recording, videotaping, or otherwise, without the prior written permission of the publisher. No one shall upload this title, or part of this title, to any social media websites.

The right of Verne Morgan to be identified as author of this work has been asserted by him in accordance with Section 77 of the Copyright, Designs and Patents Act 1988

CHARACTERS

IMMORTALS
Fairy Sugar Plum
King Rat
Father Neptune, the Old Man of the Sea

MORTALS
Dick Whittington
Mouser the Cat
Alderman Fitzwarren
Alice Fitzwarren
Sarah the Cook
Idle Jack
Captain Fairweather
Captain's Mate
Sultan of Barbary
Sentinel
Cryer
Sword-bearer ⎫ These parts can be doubled
Lord Chamberlain ⎬ by members of the chorus
Late Lord Mayor
Flunkey ⎭

Choristers—peasants, dignitaries, Lords and Ladies
Dancers
Children

ACT 1
- SCENE 1 Highgate Hill
- SCENE 2 On the way to London
- SCENE 3 Fitzwarren's General Store

ACT 2
- SCENE 1 Full Sail to Morocco
- SCENE 2 The Cruel Sea
- SCENE 3 Aboard the Raft
- SCENE 4 Sultan's Palace of Barbary
- SCENE 5 A Corridor
- SCENE 6 The Guildhall, London

MUSIC PLOT

ACT I

		Page
Opening Number (1) *Bells of St Mary* (2) *The Irish Washerwoman*	Company and Dancers	1
Turn Again Whittington	Chorus	2
Incidental—**Alice** entrance music		3
Incidental—**Jack** entrance music		3
Song	Alice and Choristers	4
Incidental—**Sarah** entrance music		4
Comedy Song	Sarah	5
Love Duet	Alice and Dick	6
Incidental—**Captain** and **Mate** entrance music		6
Comedy Duet	Captain and Mate	7
Picnic Ballet (or full Production Number)	Dancers/Company	8
Incidental—scene change		11
Song	Dick	14
Bright Opening Number	Company	14
Comedy Trio	Dick, Sarah, Jack	18
Love Duet	Dick and Alice	20
Cat Lullaby	Sarah and Mouser	22
Finale Chorus	Company	24

ACT II

Naval Number	Dick, Chorus, Dancers	26
Naval Number (reprise)		29
Hornpipe (entrance and possibly dance)	Mouser	29
Duet	Dick, and Alice with Mouser	30
Storm Music		33
Quartet—*A Life On The Ocean Wave* (can be unaccompanied)	Captain, Mate, Jack and Fitzwarren	34
A Life On the Ocean Wave (reprise)		35
Duet	Sarah and Neptune	35
Song	Dick	37
Production Number	Chorus	38
Eastern Dance	Dancers	38
Quartet	Sarah, Jack, Captain, Mate	39
Incidental—fight music		41
Production Number	Company	43
Song	Fairy	43
Community Chorus Song	Sarah and Idle Jack	44
Old Time Madrigal	Company	44
Production Number	Dick and Company	45
Concerted Item	Sarah, Fitzwarren, Jack Captain and Mate	47
Cat Ballet (or dance speciality)	Dancers	47
March Down (to include few bars of Wedding March)		47
Finale Chorus	Full Company	48

For your programme

THE STORY OF DICK WHITTINGTON
(*According to the legend*)

It all happened way back in the fourteenth century. A poor down-and-out scullion found work and shelter in the house of one Sir Ivor Fitzwaryn (so spelt in those days), Sir Ivor being a prosperous London merchant who ran a large general store in Cheapside.

It was his usual custom to send his employees in turn with a cargo of merchandise to the East. Dick, meantime, had befriended one of the household cats, and when his turn came he decided to take the cat with him for company. On one occasion, when trading with the Sultan of Barbary, he discovered that the royal palace was plagued with rats, so suggested he fetched his cat from the ship. The Sultan had never before seen such an animal. He was intrigued, and eventually purchased the cat from Dick for a vast sum of money.

This enabled Dick to set up business on his own account, and in time he became one of the richest merchants in the city. He later married his former employer's daughter, Alice, whom he had fallen in love with many years before. In 1397 he was proclaimed Lord Mayor of London, an honour which he accepted no less than three times in all. He died in 1423, leaving his entire fortune to charity.

V.M.

PRODUCTION NOTES

Costumes

Dick's first costume should not be elaborate, and in Act 1 he carries his stick over his shoulder to which is attached the traditional handkerchief-bundle. He should not change his costume till Act 2 when he can wear a naval ensemble. After he becomes rich of course anything goes. **Sarah's** mermaid make-up should consist of a flesh-pink leotard with two huge shells for the upper part, pink tights, and the tail can be easily made out of any light material or foam rubber, strapped round her waist, and coloured silvery-green. A wig of long green hair if possible, and perhaps flippers on her feet. **Neptune** should be in green with traditional flowing costume. **Mouser** should be a "pretty" cat.

The **Choristers** can wear peasant costumes for the first act, they *can* change to naval for Act 2, scene 1, and also to Eastern for Act 2, scene 4, but this is not essential. They must however wear the right type of thing in Act 2, scene 6 when they become lords and ladies, and special costumes for the small part people: Cryer, Sword-bearer, Lord Chamberlain, Late Lord Mayor, also the Flunkey unless he is doubled with the Cryer.

The **Dancers** costume plot can more or less follow the Choristers, plus any obvious speciality, such as cat make-ups for the Cat ballet (if used).

Properties

The **lifeboat** in Act 2, scene 2, can be made out of a "flat" or length of hardboard. About six to seven feet long, shaped and painted like a boat, which can have a loose piece of material attached to the bottom to represent waves and hide the occupants' feet. Four handles inside for them to slide the boat along. The oars need to be no longer than about three to four feet, and can protrude through holes cut in the sides of the boat. The **raft** should have a pole in the middle with a small flag attached.

The **soufflé** in the Picnic scene should be large and made up of a thick wet substance in order to get a good "splash".

Sound effects

For details and catalogue write to Samuel French Ltd, Sound Effects department. The more effects in the storm scene the more realistic and exciting it will be. Samuel French Ltd can also supply church bell effects on record, and these will greatly enhance the general atmosphere in scene 1.

A microphone off-stage will be useful throughout. The announcements at the end of the production can be done by this method if preferred, thus dispensing with the Flunkey.

Some **music** will be found at the end of the book which should prove a helpful guide to some items.

ACT I

Scene 1

Highgate Hill

A brightly-coloured scene, with trees and flowers, possibly a hedgerow. There is a milestone upstage with "London—5 Miles" on it. In the far distance can be seen the roofs of the houses of London Town, with here and there a tall steeple rising majestically in the hot sunny afternoon. It is mid-summer's day and the villagers are celebrating the holiday strolling about in ones and twos singing

SONG

The song should be brightly sung, if possible with harmony. The number then seques to the following jig in which Dick Whittington enters followed by the Cat

SONG

Chorus

So to Highgate Hill there came Dick Whittington,
And a cat with the wit of a kitten, and
Just as Dick was thinking of quitting he
Tarried and turned at the sound of Bow Bells.

The Choristers sing with deliberation as Dick and the Cat wend their way through the groups, uncertain which way to go. The chorus is repeated at a slightly quicker tempo, the Choristers beginning to show some animosity towards Dick, and a further chorus is repeated with some acceleration in which they close in and harass him, one of them taking a flying kick at the Cat

The Choristers hustle Dick and the Cat off as the chorus comes to its end

The Dancers enter

DANCE (*Irish Washerwoman*)

A bright, country jig. As much of the music may be used as the choreographer desires and if wished a seque back to the first number with a different style of dance to fit the tempo

The Choristers may enter for a big vocal finish at the Producer's discretion

Everyone exits at the end of the Dance

Dick enters, followed by the Cat, and strolls up to the milestone and sits

Dick (*seeing the Cat*) I do wish you wouldn't keep following me about.
Cat (*pitifully*) Mee-ow, mee-ow!

Dick What? You're hungry? So am I!
Cat (*sorrowfully*) Meeee-ow!
Dick Now don't be silly. You've followed me all the way from London. I keep telling you I'm on my way back to Gloucester. There's no work in London, I've tramped the streets from end to end. No-one wants a poor scullion like me. No work, no home, no food. I'm just down and out!

The stage lights dim, and Fairy Sugar Plum appears in a halo of amber light. She stands by Dick's side as she looks down at him

Good heavens! Who, who are you?
Fairy I'm Fairy Sugar Plum. I heard your cry of distress and I've come to help you.
Dick A fairy? A *real* fairy?
Fairy Yes, I'm real enough, as you can see.
Dick I didn't think there were such things.
Fairy Dick, you must go back to London, straight away.
Dick But London had nothing to offer me, that's why I turned and came back.
Fairy Then you must turn again. Fame and fortune is awaiting you.

Bells begin to ring off stage

Can you hear the bells?
Dick Yes, I can. I can indeed!
Fairy Hark to their message.

Offstage the Choristers sing the traditional melody, continuing quietly until their entrance

Choristers (*off*) Turn again, Whittington,
    Thou worthy citizen,
    Turn again Whittington,
    Lord Mayor of London.

The Fairy makes an unobtrusive exit

Dick Lord Mayor of London? Absurd! How could I ever become ...

The stage lights come up to full

Dick (*rising*) Why, she's gone! (*Addressing the Cat*) Did you hear what she said?

The Cat nods enthusiastically

Fame and fortune, she said. Lord Mayor of London, she said. Oh, pussy-cat! You've brought me luck! Here, tell me, what's your name?
Cat Mow-wow-ow!
Dick Mouser? What a wonderful name for a cat. And what a wonderful cat for such a name!

Mouser nods his head and jumps up and down with delight

Act I, Scene 1

Come, Cat Mouser, we'll find a nice grassy bank, rest and regain our strength, and then start the long trudge back to London.

The Choristers enter

SONG (reprise)

The music seques to a repeat chorus of Song 1 which is sung double-forte by the Choristers. Their attitude is now friendly. They smile and shake hands with Dick whilst some stroke the Cat

Dick and the Cat exit at the close of the chorus

Alderman Fitzwarren enters

Fitzwarren Good afternoon everybody!
All Good afternoon Alderman Fitzwarren!
Fitzwarren What a lovely mid-summer's day it is to be sure. Are you all enjoying the holiday?
All Yes, thank you!
Fitzwarren Has anyone seen my daughter Alice?
All No.
Fitzwarren Strange! She sat next to me in the wagon all the way from London. Then she disappeared.

Alice enters

Alice (*as she enters*) Daddy, daddy! Here I am.
Fitzwarren My daughter! I was beginning to get quite worried about you.
Alice I stopped to buy some pretty things at the goldsmiths. Look at this lovely necklace. (*She holds it aloft for him to see*)
Fitzwarren Beautiful my dear, beautiful! Its brightness makes me feel faint.
Alice Perhaps you *will* faint Daddy, when you see the bill. (*She hands it to him*)
Fitzwarren Good grief! (*He staggers*) I'll pop into the *Horse and Hounds* for a drop of mulled sack. Oh dear, I feel quite faint!

Fitzwarren exits

The Choristers now go into small conversational groups

Alice I wonder what on earth has happened to Idle Jack.

Idle Jack enters

Jack Did I hear my name mentioned?
Alice Yes Jack, you did. You were supposed to chaperone me to the goldsmith. What became of you?
Jack Oh miss, I fell asleep underneath the wagon.
Alice Under the wagon? Don't you mean inside the wagon?
Jack No miss! Y'see, I was sitting astride the horse, and I must have dropped off.
Alice Oh Jack, you really are idle! You're always sleeping.

Jack I know! Isn't it terrible! And I snore too.
Alice You snore?
Jack (*coyly*) Yes, I snore!
Alice (*after a pause*) Very loudly?
Jack Ever so! D'you know, last night I snored so loudly I kept waking myself up.
Alice What did you do?
Jack I moved into another bedroom so I couldn't hear myself.
Alice Now look, my father's brought us on our annual trip to Highgate, all the way from London. I do hope you're going to keep awake for the picnic.
Jack Oh yes miss. I never neglect the inner man no matter how tired the outer man may be.
Alice Then make your way back to the waggon and begin to unload the picnic hampers.
Jack Very good miss. (*He exits*)

SONG

Everyone exits at the end of the song

Sarah enters

A few bars of "Irish Washerwoman" should herald her entrance. She runs round the stage looking nervously over her shoulder and comes to a stop to address the audience

Sarah Oh dear, oh dear! I've been chased!... I have!... What d'you mean "I'm too old for it"?... It wasn't a man who chased me, it was —you're never going to believe this—it was a C A T! It was!... A great big cat, tremendous! It was about as big as, as... (*She measures in each direction with her hands*) About as big as... My arms aren't long enough to show you. I've never seen such a whopper. I went up to a policeman, I said "Excuse me, is it lucky or unlucky to be followed by a cat?" He said, "It depends whether you're a man or a mouse." I said, "Well, I'm neither, I'm a girl." He said, "You could have fooled me." Of course these Highgate policemen are very doodle y'know. Well of course, they see so many nanny-goats and mangey-ridden sheep, they don't recognize a nice bit of Canterbury lamb when they come across it. I'm Sarah, by the way. I work for Alderman Fitzwarren at his General store in Cheapside. I'm his cook. I've been busy all the week preparing special dishes for our picnic today. Of course, some of 'em are never satisfied, last year the Alderman tore me off a strip, "Sarah," he says, "there's no rum in this rum pie." "Well," I says, "you wouldn't expect to find a dog in a dog biscuit, would you?" I said to him this morning, "What do you suggest I take to go with the steak and kidney pie?" He said, "If it's anything like last year's I suggest you take a hammer and chisel." Mind you, had I known there were cats roaming Highgate Hill I could have made 'em a rabbit pie! Do you like cats?... Do you?... Tell you what, I'll pretend to be a cat, and you pretend to be a dog.

Act I, Scene 1

Look, every time I see you I'll go MEE-OW, and you screech back WUFF-WUFF! Will you do that, eh? Let's try it for size. (*Sarah dashes up-stage and then minces down-stage in imitation of a cat. She looks hard at audience and goes MEE-OW! After audience response she glares at them.*) That's no good! That wouldn't frighten a new born kitten let alone a hard-bitten old moggy like me! Now we'll do it again, and this time let's hear it.

After the audience response has been built up, Sarah sings her song

SONG

As Sarah takes applause at the end of her number Mouser enters and chases her round the stage and off

Alice enters in the middle of the chase and watches the fun. Dick enters immediately after

Alice (*bending and stroking Mouser*) What a lovely pussy!
Dick I'm so sorry. Did my cat scare you?
Alice Not at all, I think he's divine. What's his name?
Dick Mouser.
Alice Mouser?
Dick Yes, he loves mice.
Alice Loves mice? (*She laughs*) Oh, I see what you mean. We could do with him at Fitzwarren's store.
Dick Where's that?
Alice In Cheapside, London.
Dick Oh really? We've just come from London, and we're now on our way back.
Alice Where do you work?
Dick Nowhere at present. But I'm hoping to get a job as soon as I return, the good Fairy said I would.
Alice The good Fairy?
Dick Yes, she said fame and fortune ... oh, what rubbish am I talking?
Alice No, no, not at all! It was lovely, do go on.
Dick Oh, it was just a silly dream I had as I sat on that very milestone.
Alice Do tell me about it, please.
Dick It was a vision. I suppose you'd call it an hallucination, a trick of the imagination.
Alice What happened?
Dick I thought I saw a fairy, you see, and ... oh you'll think me crazy.
Alice (*quite seriously*) I believe in fairies.
Dick (*incredulously*) You do?
Alice Yes, I do.
Dick Well, the bells were ringing, and they seemed to say "Turn again Whittington, Lord Mayor of London". And then this fairy, she called herself Fairy Sugar Plum, appeared by the side of me—or so it seemed. "Go back," she said, "turn and go back, fame and fortune is awaiting you."
Alice So you decided to go back?

Dick Yes, and try again.
Alice What's your name?
Dick Dick Whittington.
Alice I'm Alice, Alice Fitzwarren. My father runs a store at Cheapside. I'm sure he would give you a job.
Dick I'll call at your store the minute I get back. (*To himself*) I wonder?
Alice Please do. Father is a very kindhearted man, we are here in Highgate on our annual outing which Father gives the staff every year. We have great fun, races, games, a picnic, oh it's lovely!
Dick I'm so glad I met you.
Alice So am I.

SONG

Throughout the singing Mouser listens intently

At the end of the number Dick and Alice exit on opposite sides, the Cat following Dick off

The Captain and Mate enter, to a few bars of "The Sailors Hornpipe"

The Mate has a ditty-bag slung over his shoulder. They dance round the stage, finishing with a "break", the Mate landing on his back

Captain Shiver me timbers! What sort of a sailor are you?
Mate (*rising and rubbing his hindquarters*) At the present moment I'm a sailor with a sore bulwark.
Captain You're supposed to be an A.B.
Mate What's an A.B.?
Captain An Able Body.
Mate I feel more like a D.B.
Captain What's a D.B.?
Mate A Dogs Body.
Captain Do you know why we've come to Highgate Hill.
Mate Yes, why?
Captain I'll tell you. We've come to Highgate Hill to meet a gent who's going to put some business in our way.
Mate What kind of business?
Captain He does trading with distant lands, and he wants a cargo of goods shipped to Morocco.
Mate What's this old cock's name.
Captain Don't call him old cock! He's an Alderman, and you call him sir. Understand? (*Shouting*) SIR!
Mate Okay. What's sir cock's name?
Captain You're hopeless! And what have you got in that ditty-bag?
Mate Some rabbits.
Captain Rabbits! Where did you get them?
Mate I've been poaching. In here are some rabbits and a potfer.
Captain Potfer? What's a potfer?
Mate To cook the rabbits in.
Captain Give me one of those rabbits.
Mate No.

Captain Ah, go on.
Mate No, not likely.
Captain Tell you what, if I can guess how many rabbits you've got in the bag—will you give me one?
Mate Okay! Look, if you can guess the number correctly I'll give you both of 'em.
Captain Right! Er . . . six!
Mate No. You lose.

Alderman Fitzwarren enters

Fitzwarren Ah! The Captain and Mate I presume?
Captain At your service Alderman Fitzwarren, all ship-shape and Bristol fashion.
Fitzwarren What have you got in that bag?
Mate Some rabbits, sir cock.
Fitzwarren We could do with one of those for our picnic today.
Mate Sorry.
Fitzwarren Oh, come on? I'll make a bargain. Give me one of those rabbits and you can come to our picnic.
Mate I've got a better idea. If you can guess how many rabbits I've got in the bag—I'll give you both of 'em.
Fitzwarren That's easy. (*He roars with laughter*)
Mate Not as easy as you think. Want to bet?
Fitzwarren (*convulsed with laughter*) Yes I'll bet. I'll have a pound.
Mate Hold your money up.
Fitzwarren (*holding up a pound note*) Two!
Mate No, six!
Fitzwarren Six? But you said if I guessed correctly you'd give me *both* of them.
Mate Yes, but rabbits breed so quickly! (*He grabs the pound note and makes to exit*)
Fitzwarren Here, just a minute. We have business to discuss. Now, what I want you to do is to take a shipment of goods to Barbary for me.
Captain (*saluting smartly*) We will be pleased to serve before the mast.
Fitzwarren Come to my store in London and we'll settle terms.
Captain Very good Mister Alderman, you scratch my back and I'll scratch yours.
Fitzwarren Yes . . . What? Oh I see what you mean.
Mate Can we come to your picnic? I haven't had a square meal for days.
Fitzwarren Oh poor man! Here's a dog biscuit for you. (*He gives him a biscuit and exits*)

SONG

It should be a bright number, if possible with audience participation

   The Captain and Mate exit at the end of the song

   The Dancers (and Choristers if required) enter

PICNIC BALLET (Dancers or full production number)

The mime portrays the laying of the tablecloth, the bringing on of the picnic basket and any other relevant properties

The Dancers exit after the dance

Alderman Fitzwarren, Idle Jack and Alice are led on by Sarah

Sarah addresses the audience as the others drop into place round the tablecloth. Jack has a fly-swat with him

Sarah MEE-OW (*She waits for audience reaction with "Wuff-Wuff" then sits at her place by the tablecloth*)
Fitzwarren Well, another year has slipped by, and once again here we all are gathered together about to enjoy our annual picnic. Regale yourselves of the goodies that Sarah has been busy preparing for the past week. Idle Jack, you say grace.
Jack Grace who?
Fitzwarren Not grace *who*! The grace we say as a thanksgiving before a meal.
Jack Oh, sorry! (*He rises*)

All bow their heads

I declare this nosh-up duly open.

The Captain and Mate enter

Captain Has the beano started?
Fitzwarren Yes, do please join in. Just ask for anything you fancy, we've got everything at this feast, everything.
Mate Did you say—everything?
Fitzwarren Yes, everything.
Mate Can I have a kangaroo on toast?
Fitzwarren A what?
Mate A kangaroo on toast.
Fitzwarren Sarah?
Sarah No kangaroo on toast. We've run out of bread.
Jack Can I have an ice cream?
Sarah We aint got none.
Jack (*mimicking*) Aint got none? Why not? We had it last year.
Sarah No we didn't.
Jack Yes we did. Look, I've got a picture of me eating ice cream at last year's picnic.
Sarah (*looking over his shoulder*) I can't see any ice cream.
Jack 'Course not, I've eaten it all.
Sarah (*snatching the card away from him and studying it closely*) I can't see you, either!
Jack Well, you don't expect me to hang about when the ice cream's gone, do you?

The Mate sips a drink from a mug and spits it out hurrieldy

Mate Good grief! What's this, tea or coffee?
Sarah What's it taste like?
Mate Paraffin!
Sarah Ah well, if it tastes like paraffin it's coffee. The tea tastes like turpentine.
Captain This pork pie's a bit tough.
Sarah I made that pork pie out of the cookery book.
Captain Reckon I've got hold of the cardboard cover.
Jack I thought you said you were going to make us a rhubarb tart this year.
Sarah I couldn't get a pie dish long enough.
Alice (*to Fitzwarren*) Have you tried the sausages?
Fitzwarren (*dryly*) Yes, and found them guilty.
Sarah Try a bit of my Handy Cake.
Alice Why do you call it Handy Cake?
Sarah A trade secret. You see, instead of baking powder I use tooth powder, so they can eat the cake and clean their teeth at the same time.
Alice (*dubiously*) How do you know when it's done.
Sarah I stick one of the kitchen knives in, if it comes out clean—it's done.
Fitzwarren Sarah! Do me a favour.
Sarah Yes, Mister Fitzwarren, sir?
Fitzwarren If the kitchen knife does come out clean, stick all the others in!

The Mate begins to cough and splutter, the Captain goes to him and slaps him vigorously on the back

Captain What's the matter?
Mate I've swallowed a frog.
Jack What's he say?
Captain Says he's swallowed a frog.
Jack Oh dear, I hope he's not going to croak.

The Mate continues to cough and the Captain continues to slap his back

Alice What's wrong?
Jack Says he's swallowed a frog.
Alice Is he choking?
Jack No, I think he's dead serious.
Alice I said "choking". Here, give him a sip of wine.

The wine bottle is passed to the Mate. He takes a sip, pauses, then coughs again. He takes a good swig, pauses, and coughs again. Then lifts the bottle and drinks heartily. The others have watched the proceedings with fascination

Jack (*suddenly going into a violent paroxism*) Oh, oh! I've swallowed a frog! Quick!

The bottle is immediately passed to Idle Jack and he drinks. The Captain suddenly rolls on his back with a shout

Captain Now *I've* swallowed a frog! Pass the bottle, quick! Quick!

As the Captain begins to drink Fitzwarren comes forward and snatches the bottle away from him

Fitzwarren Half that wine was supposed to be for Alice and me.
Captain Yes guv, but y'see, our half was at the bottom.

Fitzwarren glares at him and prepares to take a good swig at the bottle. There is the noise of a bee humming. They all begin to look upwards and Sarah pretends to flick the bee off the food. Jack picks up the fly-swat and follows the bee around with a stealthy walk, looking upwards. Fitzwarren by now has got the bottle at the perpendicular and is taking a long satisfying drink as Jack approaches. He gives him a mighty whack on the back with the fly-swat. Fitzwarren chokes copiously, and the others gather round, smacking his back with such heartiness they half-kill him in the process

Sarah (*as things begin to settle down*) That'll teach you not to be so fond of the wine gums!
Fitzwarren (*looking daggers at Sarah*) This picnic is beginning to remind me of that old Scotch motto.
Sarah What Scotch motto?
Fitzwarren Dinner forget!
Sarah (*brightly*) Oh don't say that Mister Fitz. Here, drink your coffee and cheer yourself up.
Fitzwarren Coffee? It tastes like mud.
Sarah Well it was only ground this morning.

Sarah thinks for a moment, then begins to laugh at her own joke. Meantime Fitzwarren with a wry face throws back his head with a view to downing his coffee at one gulp. Simultaneously Sarah in her hilarity gives him a hefty slap on the back. Fitzwarren chokes again

Alice Daddy dear, did you hear that funny story about a man who had a picnic in the jungle?
Fitzwarren (*in embittered voice*) No, I don't know it.
Alice It's so funny, I'm sure it will make you laugh.
Sarah Tell us it then, make Mister Fitzwarren laugh, go on!
Alice Well you see, it goes like this: "Something he disagreed with—ate him!"

There is stony silence while they all look hard at Fitzwarren. Fitzwarren, pan-faced, looks straight ahead. After about three seconds they each relax and raise their coffee cups to their lips. Just as they commence to drink Fitzwarren lets forth an enormous shout of laughter. They all choke

Sarah (*to Jack*) How do you like your hash?
Jack My what?
Sarah Your hash.
Jack That's a good name for it.
Sarah (*to Alice*) No good expecting praise from Jack, he doesn't know putty from porridge.
Fitzwarren No wonder his windows fall out.

Act I, Scene 2

Jack And I'll tell you something else I don't like.
Sarah What's that?
Jack I can't stand cheese with holes in it.
Sarah Oh, don't be so fussy! Just eat the cheese and leave the holes on the side of your plate.
Mate (*handing Jack a small potato chip*) Here you are, Jacky-boy. Have a micro chip.
Sarah He's got one—on his shoulder! If opportunity knocked he'd complain about the noise.
Alice Come on everybody, I want to take a photograph of you.

Alice comes down stage with the camera, the others get into a group centre stage

Fitzwarren You would! Just when I was about to enjoy my souffle!
Alice Doesn't matter, bring the souffle with you.

Fitzwarren carries the souffle and sits with it on his lap as he squats in the centre of the group

Fitzwarren My favourite dish! I've been looking forward to it all the morning.
Sarah (*coyly*) I made it specially for the Alderman.
Alice Now! Dead still everyone.

There is the hum of another bee. In spite of themselves they begin to look upwards, following the flight of the bee with heads going right and left, all except Fitzwarren who is applying himself religiously to the souffle whilst trying to smile into the camera at the same time

Alice Now do please keep still, all of you! It's a three second exposure. Father: Look at the camera!

Jack picks up the fly-swat and is stalking the bee. Just as Alice takes the shot Jack makes a large swipe at the bee, brings the fly-swat down firmly on the souffle, shattering it in all directions

Black-out

The music strikes up for scene change (*bright number or reprise*)

SCENE 2

On the way to London. A street scene on front cloth or tabs

The scene opens in complete darkness. A red spot picks up King Rat as he enters

Rat   Know who I am?
              I bet you don't.
              My name, it is a good'n,
              I don't tell everybody it,
              I'm not such a silly pudd'n.

He looks off-stage, then back to audience

> Okay, here goes! I'll tell you then,
> Although you'll think me bats,
> (*Pompously*) I am the King of the Rats, I am,
> And (*viciously*) I DON'T LIKE CATS!
> A chap called Whittington's roaming around,
> In blouse and ragged trouser,
> He's got a cat, so I've been told,
> A mangey old thing called Mouser.
> I'll dine on that cat tomorrow night,
> I'll have him with "tomarters",
> I'll drink his blood
> And chew the cud,
> And have his guts for starters!
> But how to catch him?
> That's the thing.
> Come on!
> Don't all look wooden.
> Thought of one yet?
> Well I have then!
> Listen, I think it's a good'n.

He looks to see if he is being overheard, then continues

> As he bends, to sniff down a mouse's hole,
> I'll jump on his back!
> And poor old soul
> His good intent will all go phut
> 'Cos I'll give him a bite
> Right through his nut.
> He will cat-er-waul,
> As is his wont,
> Then, I'll finish him off,
> You see if I don't.

Fairy Sugar Plum enters R. *She is picked up by a White Lime*

Fairy	Oh no you won't!
Rat	Oh yes I will!
Fairy	You won't!
Rat	I will!
	And who are you?
Fairy	*I'm* Fairy Sugar Plum
	Good and true.
Rat	Well, don't interfere,
	Mind your own biz.
Fairy	I will indeed,
	My biz it is!
	Your evil, I'll pursue it,

Act I, Scene 2

	For I have fairy-magic! Yes
	And *I'll* see you don't do it.
Rat	Fairy who, did you say you are?
Fairy	(*proudly*) Sugar Plum!
Rat	Oh, my gracious!
	A fairy with a name like that
	Must be most efficatious.
Fairy	I am, and what is more my friend
	You'd best not over-do it,
	You let that little Cat alone
	Or else the day you'll rue it.
Rat	(*Accepting the challenge*)
	Right! Now to you I say "Adieu".
Fairy	And I say Boo! to you.
Rat	And I say Pooh! to you.
Fairy	Your Pooh! I Boo!
Rat	Your Boo! I Pooh!
BOTH	And the same to *you*!
Fairy	And I hope you catch the cat flu!

King Rat exits

Fairy (*addressing the audience*)
    Don't worry little ones,
    Your story's safe with me.
    I'll follow this cat
    From London Town
    To the shores of Barbary.
    I'll guard him and Dick
    Every inch of the way,
    You'll support me, this I trow,
    Will you? . . . Please! . . .
    I'm *sure* you will.
    Hush! They're coming—now!

The Fairy exits R

Dick and Mouser enter L

Dick Come on Mouser. We're nearly there. Only another three miles.

Mouser is limping along behind and eventually drops to the floor exhausted

    Oh, poor old Mouser! You're absolutely exhausted, aren't you?

Mouser nods his head wearily

    Never mind. I'm sure we'll get work at Fitzwarren's store. Wasn't she a lovely lady—Alice, I mean.

Mouser nods happily

    Did you like her?

Mouser nods vigorously

Do you . . . do you think she's pretty?

Mouser goes coy and buries his head

I wonder if the boys and girls think she's pretty? Do you? . . . Do you think Alice is pretty? . . . Yes, I think so too. But we mustn't call her Alice to her face, you know. She's the boss's daughter. We must call her—Miss Fitzwarren. And Mouser, you must bow to her. Like this! (*Dick executes an exaggerated stately bow*) Yes, you must! Go on now, try it.

Mouser rises, hesitates, then does a quick little jerky bow

Oh no! That's no use at all. Alice . . . I mean, Miss Fitzwarren, will never be impressed. I'll show you again. (*Dick repeats the courtly bow*)

Mouser makes two or three attempts but doubles up with laughter. Eventually he gets the hang of it and repeats it two or three times

Splendid! Now remember, every time we see Miss Fitzwarren you do that. Understand?

Mouser nods his head and performs another graceful bow, as Dick goes into his song

SONG

The lights fade at the end of the number as the music strikes up for the opening of the next scene

SCENE 3

Fitzwarren's General Store

Interior of a well-stocked shop. Two counters at an angle are placed up-stage. Centre stage is a large safe. Displayed at the producer's discretion are various commodities, anything to give the impression of a busy store. The Backcloth represents period windows facing outwards towards the street

At Curtain rise Idle Jack is serving behind one counter. Sarah behind the other. The customers (Choristers) are milling around singing the opening number, examining goods etc.

SONG

The Dancers can be brought into the number if wished

Alderman Fitzwarren enters as the song finishes

Fitzwarren (*coming to centre stage*) Good morning customers.
All Good morning Alderman Fitzwarren.
Fitzwarren I now declare this store duly open. Buy, buy, buy! And remember, we sell everything in this store from a pin to an elephant!
All Ooooh!

The customers begin to exit as the dialogue begins. The following scene

Act I, Scene 3

should be worked quickly and brightly, one customer entering as the other exits. The customers voices should be kept up almost to the point of shouting

1st Lady (*approaching Fitzwarren*) I want some soap.

Alderman Fitzwarren waves her across to Idle Jack

(*To Jack*) Some soap please.
Jack (*to the lady*) Yes, would you like it scented?
1st Lady No thank you, I'll take it with me. (*She exits*)
1st Man (*indicating a small paper bag*) These moth balls you sold me are no good.
Fitzwarren Why not?
1st Man I haven't hit a single moth with them. (*He exits*)
Small Girl (*sidling up to Fitzwarren*) 'Ere, I've got jelly in this ear and custard in this one.
Fitzwarren Well what do you want?
Small Girl Eh?
Fitzwarren I said, what d'you want?
Small girl You'll have to speak up, I'm a trifle deaf.
Fitzwarren (*shouting*) What do you want?
Small Girl Some nappies for our new baby.

Fitzwarren motions her over to Sarah

Sarah Here you are. That's two pounds for the nappies and thirty pence for the tax.
Small Girl Oh, don't bother about the tax. Mother uses safety pins.

Sarah throws the packet at her as the girl runs off

2nd Lady (*entering at speed passing Fitzwarren and going straight up to Idle Jack*) I'm in a hurry! I want a mousetrap.
Jack Yes madam, what kind of mousetrap?
2nd Lady Any kind. Hurry up, I want to catch a train.
Jack Oh, I'm afraid we haven't got one that big.

2nd Lady exits quickly as 2nd Man enters

2nd Man (*to Fitzwarren*) I want some pepper please.
Fitzwarren Yes sir, white pepper or brown pepper?
2nd Man No, writing pepper. (*He exits*)

3rd Lady enters and hurries straight up to Idle Jack

3rd Lady Young man! Have you got a sheep's head?
Jack No lady, it's the way I part my hair.

3rd Lady exits

4th Lady (*carrying pencil and long sheet of paper, enters and goes up to Sarah*) Excuse me, I'm doing a survey on politics. What do you think of Red China?

Sarah (*resting casually on the counter*) Well, you know, I think it looks nice on a white tablecloth, don't you?

4th Lady exits in disgust

3rd Man enters at great speed. He wears a mask, has his hat pulled well down over his eyes, and points a pistol

3rd Man Don't move anybody! This is a hold-up!

Everyone raises their hands

(*Strolling over to Idle Jack*) Give me your money or I'll shoot you.

Jack Ah well, you'd better shoot me then, I shall need the money for my old age.

3rd Man (*lowering his pistol*) Ah yes, I never thought of that. (*To Fitzwarren, on his way out*) Er, could you lend me a fiver on my Access card?

Fitzwarren Get out of it! (*He shushes him off*)

5th Lady enters

5th Lady (*going to Sarah*) Yesterday you gave me soapflakes for cornflakes, and my husband had 'em for breakfast.

Sarah Oh dear! Was he cross?

5th Lady Cross? He was foaming at the mouth.

5th Lady exits

4th Man (*going to Fitzwarren*) Do you have frog's legs?

Fitzwarren No, the rheumatism makes me walk this way.

4th Man exits

Idle Jack leaves his counter and approaches Fitzwarren

Jack It's no good, I can't go on any longer, Mister Fitzwarren.

Fitzwarren Why, what's the matter Idle Jack?

Jack I keep on thinking I'm a goat.

Fitzwarren A goat? How long have you had this feeling?

Jack Ever since I was a kid.

Sarah (*coming down from her counter*) Yesterday he kept on thinking he was a chicken.

Fitzwarren I know, he's always thinking he's a chicken.

Sarah Well, why don't you take him to a psychiatrist?

Fitzwarren I would, but we need the eggs.

Sarah You see, it's very catching. All morning I've been thinking I'm a pair of curtains.

Fitzwarren Well, why don't you pull yourself together?

Sarah The trouble with Jack, he's idle.

Jack Oh, I wouldn't say that.

Sarah Yes you are, you're idle, Jack.

Jack I know I'm Idle Jack, but I'm not idle.

Sarah You are so idle if you walked any slower you'd be going backwards.

Act I, Scene 3

Fitzwarren Now that's enough, the pair of you! Get busy down below, there's a customer coming.

Sarah and Idle Jack exit glaring at each other

Dick and Cat enter from the street door

Dick (*with a bow*) Good morning, sir.
Fitzwarren Didn't you see that notice outside?
Dick What notice?
Fitzwarren No dogs!
Dick This isn't a dog, it's a cat.
Fitzwarren Smelly things, cats.
Dick I'm looking for good honest work sir, I'm hungry.
Fitzwarren Why don't you skin the cat? (*He laughs uproariously at his joke*)

Mouser chases him round the stage. Fitzwarren withdraws behind the counter

Dick Mouser! Behave! I'm sorry sir. Like me, the cat's hungry.
Fitzwarren (*apprehensively*) Tell him to go outside and have a roll on the lawn!
Dick Sir, if you will only give me a job, I promise you will never regret it.
Fitzwarren (*sizing him up*) H'm! I could do with an extra hand in the shop. But you'd have to get rid of the cat.
Dick Oh sir, I couldn't do that. Couldn't you take him on as a mouser.
Fitzwarren A mouser?
Dick Yes, that's his name, he's a wonderful mouser. Have you any mice, sir?
Fitzwarren More than our share down in the basement.
Dick Then Mouser's your man. He'll soon clear them out.
Fitzwarren Really? Got sharp teeth, has he?
Dick Oh yes!
Fitzwarren (*backing away a little*) Ah! Thought so. D'you know, I rather like you. You have an honest face. I *will* take you on—and the cat.
Dick Oh sir!
Fitzwarren And to prove my trust in you, here is the spare key to the safe. Guard it with your life. And while you mind the shop I'll take Tiddles downstairs and introduce him to his new mousy friends.

Fitzwarren and Mouser exit

Idle Jack enters

Jack Oh, hallo! Who are you?
Dick My name's Dick.
Jack My name's Jack.
Dick How do you do, Jack?
Jack How do you do, Dick?
Dick I like the name of Jack.
Jack Do you? Fitzwarren calls me Idle Jack, 'cause he reckons I'm lazy.
Dick I'm sure that's not true.

Jack It is y'know. I'm always sleeping. One day I went to sleep sitting on the bacon slicer.
Dick Oh dear, what happened?
Jack I got a little behind with my orders. (*He busies himself behind the counter*)

Sarah enters

Sarah Hallo, who are you?
Dick I'm Dick Whittington, the new apprentice.
Sarah Do you know anything about making bread?
Dick A little, yes.
Sarah Very well then, why is a woman like dough?
Dick I don't know. Why *is* a woman like dough?
Sarah Because you need her dear, you *need* her! (*She roars with laughter*)

Jack moves towards Dick and Sarah

Jack (*to Dick*) 'Scuse me, why is a woman like dough?
Dick This lady has just told me; it's because you *need* her.
Jack No, because she's hard to get off your hands!

Jack and Sarah cling on to each other as they roar their heads off

Jack Tell me something, Dick.
Dick What?
Jack Who was the first butcher?
Dick The first butcher? 'Fraid I don't know.
Jack Adam.
Dick Adam?
Jack Yes, Adam!... Because...
Sarah } *together* { He exchanged a rib for a bit of skirt!
Jack
Dick You're having me on, aren't you?
Sarah (*trying to control her laughter*) I suppose you know his name was Jack.
Dick Who's name?
Sarah Adam.
Dick Adam?
Sarah Yes! Y'see, first there was Jack Adam, then there was Eve Adam, and now we've all got 'em!

All three laugh heartily

Excuse me, may I be pardoned while I try something for size?
Dick Certainly.

Sarah walks to the footlights, looks at the audience, and bellows "MEE-OW!" After audience participation they go into their song

SONG

They exit after their number

The Stage lights dim. There is a magnesium flash and King Rat enters. He is picked up by a Red Lime

Act I, Scene 3

Rat So Dick's got a job here,
With that cat,
They'll live happy ever after,
I don't doubt that.
With all this food
They'll soon be besotted,
I wish 'em no harm but
I hope their cream gets clotted.

King Rat exits

The lights come up to full again

Dick enters, followed by Mouser

He walks briskly to behind the counter

Mouser squats in a chair

Dick My word, aren't I lucky? Got a job here right away. I hope we get lots and lots of customers so that I can work ever so hard and make Alderman Fitzwarren proud of me. Hallo, here comes a customer right now.

Alice enters

Alice Ah, good morning.
Dick Good morning madam, can I help you?
Alice Why, it's Dick!
Dick Alice! Er, I'm sorry, Miss Fitzwarren. Mouser, Mouser, *bow*!

Mouser jumps off the chair and gives a bow to Alice

Alice (*pretending a curtsy*) How delightful! So you are both installed. I knew Father would be sympathetic.
Dick Can I serve you, Miss Fitzwarren.
Alice Yes you can, you can serve me best by calling me Alice, like everyone else does.
Dick Very well Miss Fitz . . . er, Alice.
Alice That's better. And Mouser, you can stop bowing and scraping to me. We are all equal here. No need to be formal.
Dick You are more than kind, Miss Alice. And Mouser, *Mouser*! Stop that silly bowing!

Mouser stops bowing and rolls at Alice's feet

Alice He's a darling. The most polite cat I've ever met.

Mouser jumps up and begins bowing again. Dick quietly pulls him away to his rear

Dick Can I get you something, Miss Alice.
Alice Yes, this lovely necklace which Father bought me in Highgate. I want you to put it in the safe.
Dick (*taking the necklace*) What a lovely necklace.

Alice Yes, it's quite valuable. Be sure you lock the safe securely.
Dick Mr Fitzwarren gave me the spare key. I keep it in my bundle, which I always keep with me for safety.

Dick unlocks the safe, puts the necklace in, returns the key to his bundle and places it on the counter

Alice I hope you will be very happy with us.
Dick I'm sure I will. Miss ... Alice! May I ask you a question?
Alice Yes, of course.
Dick Do you believe in love at first sight.
Alice I don't know, I've never really thought about it.
Dick Well, think about it now.

SONG

At the end of the duet Alice exits one side, Dick and Mouser the other. Alice gives him a little wave on her exit and Dick blows her a kiss, completely forgetting his bundle which he leaves on the counter

Fitzwarren enters followed by Idle Jack

Fitzwarren is holding three bags of gold in his hands. Each is about the size of a tennis ball

Fitzwarren Now listen to me Idle Jack. I have three bags of gold here. I want you to put them in the safe for me. (*He hands the bags of gold to Jack*) Now Jack, I put three bags of gold in the safe yesterday, and three bags the day before, so with those how many bags of gold have we got?
Jack Eight!
Fitzwarren Now don't be silly. Three three's are nine, aren't they children?
Jack No, three three's are eight. Aren't they children?
Fitzwarren You see! Every little boy and girl knows that three three's are nine.
Jack You've all made a boo-boo, and I'll prove it to you.

Jack places the three bags of gold on the floor. He picks up the first two bags saying as he does so "One, two." He leaves the third bag on the floor and points to it as he says "three". He then puts down by the side of it a bag as he counts "four" and another by the side of that as he counts "five". (All three bags are now on the floor). He then picks up each bag one at a time, counting as he does so "six, seven, eight"

Jack There y'are! Told you, three three's are eight.

Sarah enters

Fitzwarren Ah, Sarah! We're having a bit of a hoo-hah! Jack has just proved to me that three three's are eight. But I'm not convinced, I think three three's are nine.
Sarah Well, you're both wrong. As a matter of the strictist multiplididdlem —three three's are eleven.
Fitzwarren Three three's are eleven? You're worse than he is!

Act I, Scene 3

Sarah And I can prove it.

Sarah takes the three bags. She throws two bags to the floor, counting "one, two" as she does so, but keeps the third bag in her hand as she counts "three". She then picks up the two bags seperately from the floor as she says "four, five". She now has all three bags in her hands. She then puts each bag on the floor one at a time as she counts "six, seven, eight", and picks each one up as she counts "nine, ten, eleven". The quicker this gag is worked the more convincing and confusing it will be

Sarah Like I said, three three's are eleven.
Fitzwarren I must be out of my tiny Cheapside mind! Give those bags to me.

Fitzwarren snatches the bags of gold from Sarah and pops them in the safe. Whilst he is doing this Sarah does her "MEE-OW" gag with the audience

Fitzwarren and Idle Jack exit

Mouser enters

In Mouser's mouth is a property mouse. He drops it on the floor and begins to play with it, dapping at it with his paw, throwing it up in the air and so on, Sarah, quite unaware of his presence, gets herself a chair and sits centre stage. Meantime she continues to gossip to the audience

Sarah Oh, it's nice to sit down. Never get a minute to myself you know. All go, that's what it is. I do the cooking, serve in the shop, warm the guv'nors bed, Oh my goodness, there's a cat! Help! Somebody come!

Mouser brings the mouse over to Sarah and drops it in her lap

Oh! A mouse! Take it away, I don't want it.

Mouser whispers something into her ear

What? Do what with the little mouse?... Put it in *where*?... I will do nothing of the sort! What kind of a cook do you think I am?

Mouser nods several times and whispers again

I repeat, I will not under any circumstances put that smelly lump of compos in today's stew. (*To the audience*) It would be different if we were having toad-in-the-hole.

Mouser whispers again

You'd like me to sing you a little lullaby? Very well, take your demised friend outside before it becomes decomposed and I'll think up something.

Sarah picks up the mouse by its tail and hands it to Mouser

Mouser goes off with the mouse and returns immediately

Isn't he a nice cat. Do you like him? I wonder who he belongs to? Who? Dick who? Really? Don't say any more...

Mouser snuggles up to Sarah and she turns a trifle coy

> Long time since a male snuggled up to me like that! Come on, come a bit closer! You do remind me of a pantomime I once saw in a chemist's shop.

Mouser shakes his head violently

> Yes, it was in a chemist's shop. It was called Puss in Boots.

Mouser laughs and gives Sarah a playful little dab. Sarah slaps him back, and Mouser returns the slap so fervently Sarah falls off the chair

SONG

Any suitable number will suffice, preferably one in which Mouser can come in with a few mee-ows

> *Sarah and Mouser exit after their song*
>
> *King Rat enters, looking around furtively*

Rat   Things are not going quite my way,
                  That Dick and his Cat are here to stay,
                  Unless, of course, he comes to grief
                  Because he's proved to be a *thief*!

(He reacts at the thought of it)

                  I say! What fun! I really must
                  Think up a scheme or I shall bust!
                  I know! . . .

(From now on he suits the action to his words)

                  I'll take the necklace from the safe
                  And stick it in his handkerchafe!
                  What? . . . Pardon? . . . Rotten rhyme?
                  So where's the crunch? It's pantomime!
                  So handkerchafe, or handker*chief*,
                  I'll prove old Dick's a dirty thief.

(He removes the necklace from the safe, and places it with the key inside Dick's bundle)

                  The deed is *done*!
                  So, suffering snakes and a He-Hi-Ho!
                  'Tis time for me to do a dido!

He makes a frisky exit

Captain and Mate enter

Captain Here we are at last. This is Fitzwarren's famous store. This is where we complete the deal.
Mate (*sniffing*) I smell a rat.
Captain Don't worry, he won't diddle me.

Act I, Scene 3

Mate No, I mean a real rat.
Captain It's probably that mangy old cat they call Mouser.

Sarah enters

Sarah Who's talking about *me*?
Captain No wonder you smelt a rat, here's Sarah.
Mate Now I smell trouble.
Sarah You're always smelling something. Perhaps you've got catarrh.
Mate I wouldn't know how to play one if I had it.
Sarah (*to Captain*) I hope your vessel's seaworthy, 'cos *he'll* never know how to drive it.
Captain Everything on my boat is shipshape and Bristol fashion.
Sarah Same with me. My shape is lovely, and my Bristols are the latest fashion.
Captain Yes, fifty years ago.
Sarah So I've decided to join your crew. When do we sail?
Captain Sorry, I don't have women aboard my ship.
Mate 'Scuse me guv'. She's the cook here, she might be useful in the galley.
Sarah I could be useful in lots of places.
Captain My crew want nourishment, not punishment.
Sarah I'll make you a Parisienne Pheasant.
Captain What's that?
Sarah A black pudding with a feather stuck in it.

Idle Jack enters

Jack Hallo sailors! How do I go about joining your ship?
Captain You don't.
Jack What?
Captain Join my ship.
Mate Say guv', we need as many men as we can get to augment this voyage to Morocco.
Captain I know, but he's no good. He hasn't the strength to lie in bed.

Dick enters

Mate Now, here's a likely lad. Ahoy there! Would you like a sea voyage to Barbary? Lovely grog, lovely girls!
Dick No thank you, I've got a good job here. I wouldn't give it up for anything in the world.

Fitzwarren and Alice enter together with the Chorus

Fitzwarren Ah, the gentlemen of the high seas. Let me settle our debt and you can set sail.

He unlocks the safe and withdraws the three bags of gold which he passes over to the Captain

Alice Oh Daddy! Look!
Fitzwarren What's the matter?
Alice My necklace, it's gone!

Fitzwarren (*dashing to the safe*) Gone? What do you mean.
Alice I gave it to Dick Whittington to put in the safe, and . . .
Fitzwarren (*to Dick*) Well, what have you done with it?
Dick I locked it in the safe, and put the key in my bundle.
Fitzwarren Where is your bundle?
Captain There it is, on the counter.
Dick Oh dear! I must have forgotten to . . .

Fitzwarren strides to the counter, picks Dick's bundle up and searches it

Fitzwarren Here it is! (*He holds the necklace aloft*) What have you to say—thief?
Dick I swear I am innocent.
Fitzwarren You had the only spare key. Get out of my store!
Dick Alice, you believe me?
Fitzwarren (*throwing the bundle at him*) Go!
Dick Very well Captain, I *will* join your ship.
Captain Good! Follow the Mate and stow your gear aboard.

Mouser enters and runs to Dick

Mate No cats aboard. Cats are unlucky!
Dick I'll come back for you Mouser, just as soon as I've made my fortune. Don't fret! I'll be back!
Mate (*shooing Mouser with his hat*) Go on Tiddles, get out of it—Shoo! . . . Get-out-of-it!

He chases Mouser off and they exit followed by Dick

Alice (*calling after him*) Dick! I believe you. Wherever you go I will follow you! Dick . . . come back!
Fitzwarren (*grabbing her arm and pulling her towards the exit*) Come, I'm going to lock you in your bedroom.

Fitzwarren and Alice exit, Alice protesting vehemently

Captain Any more volunteers?
Chorus Yes! All of us! Hurrah!

FINALE CHORUS

This should be something in keeping with the situation, preferably a "sailaway" chorus.

> *Jack and Sarah exit and return immediately carrying luggage; Jack a kitbag and Sarah a quantity of paper parcels*

> *The Mate and Dick return and join in the finale singing*

> *As the chorus draws to a close the Mate leads the other Principals off*

> *Alice enters in hat and coat, carrying a smart case. As she exits at a trot Fitzwarren enters doing a knees-up run, arms in the manner of a runner, following her*

Act I, Scene 3

The Curtain falls with a flamboyant picture by the Chorus and Dancers
Curtain Call is Mouser seen scurrying across the stage in pursuance of his master

CURTAIN

ACT II

Scene 1

Full Sail To Morocco

The scene represents the upper deck of a ship. The bulwarks stretch from side to side up-stage. There is a small space between them and the sky-cloth. Any other accoutrements according to stage facilities

SONG

This should be a bright production number, possibly led by Dick, who is now in a smart naval costume

The Dancers enter and, as a suggestion, can perform a "Signal Dance" with small flags. Some can carry mops on long poles and mime the holystoning of the deck to rhythm, etc. The girls are dressed in fancy naval attire

   At the end of the number the Captain enters

Captain Company! Fall in!

The Dancers form a straight line centre stage, any others exit. Dick takes up a position at the end of the line

   The Mate enters and falls into line

   Sara enters, carrying a bucket and mop. She is dressed in somewhat bizarre naval attire

   Alderman Fitzwarren enters, also in naval attire

Captain Now then, now then! Fall into line. Stand to attention!
Sarah (*to audience*) MEE-OW! (*To Captain*) Are we all here yet?
Captain Who are you?
Sarah I'm Sarah, the cook, remember?
Captain Then go to the galley and put your chops in the oven.
Sarah Put my chops in the oven? For two pins I'd freeze your assets.
Captain Don't speak to me.
Sarah You're speaking to me.
Captain Do you know who I am?
Sarah Do you?
Captain Of course I do.
Sarah Well what are you asking me for?

   Idle Jack enters wearing an ill-fitting sailor suit and carrying a large box on his shoulder

Captain Hey you! What are you doing on deck with that box?

Act II, Scene 1

Jack I suffer with sleepy sickness and I'm using this iron box to rest my weary head on.
Sarah Bit hard for a pillow isn't it?
Jack Not when I stuff it with feathers it won't be.
Captain Put it on the poop you nincompoop.
Jack (*throwing the box off-stage*) I'm tired, I've had no sleep since I woke up.
Captain You'll get precious little sleep on this ship. Get into line, I'll give you your orders.
Jack Please yourself, I shan't take 'em.
Captain Firstly, you rise at three o'clock every morning.
Sarah (*unable to believe her ears*) Did you say morning?
Captain *Morning!*
Sarah (*making for the exit*) Good afternoon.
Jack (*also making for the exit*) Good evening.
Mate That's another day gone!
Captain Come back, both of you.

Sarah and Jack return to the line

You tumble out of your bunk at five minutes to three.
Jack And bunk back at five past.
Captain Then you run to work . . .
Jack Run? To work?
Captain And then you get on your knees and scrub the deck.
Sarah (*after a pause*) Just a minute! What about you, what do you do?
Captain Me? I give the orders.
Sarah You're the captain?
Captain Yes, I'm the captain.
Sarah It's your ship?
Captain My ship.
Sarah All of it?
Captain All of it.
Sarah Well scrub it yourself!

She thrusts the bucket and mop into the Captain's hands. Then walks back to her place in the line. The Captain, bordering on a state of apoplexy, follows her and hurls the bucket and mop back at her

Captain Understand! I won't have it.
Sarah Well bung it over there.

She flings the bucket and mop to the other side of the stage. The Mate steps forward to support the Captain who is sagging at the knees

Captain (*weakly*) I've never been so flabbergasted!
Mate Yes guv', and I'm flabbergasted.
Sarah Two gasted flabbers for the price of one.
Captain (*pulling himself together*) Silence! Straighten up the line! We'll now do some drill.

Everyone shuffles into line and stands to attention

Company... wait for it, wait for it... Mark time!

They all mark time quite smartly, except Idle Jack who, though keeping in step, executes a curiously high elevation, literally "leaping" up and down with enormous energy

(*almost speechless*) Company! HALT!

They halt, and there is an expectant pause. Idle Jack then collapses, toppling over from the waist with his head dangling, from sheer exhaustion

Sarah Oh dear, he's feeling seasick, quick!

Sarah runs and gets the bucket which she places under Idle Jack's head

Come on old boy, pull yourself to pieces! I'll see you home.

Sarah moves the bucket out of the way then grabs Idle Jack by the scruff of the neck and tries to straighten him up. Each time he falls back to the dangling position. Sarah gets the mop and props him up by placing the end of the handle under his nose with the mop-head taking the strain on the floor

The Captain, who has not witnessed the business, suddenly sees the spectacle and is overtly appalled

Captain Here I say! Take it away! Go on, *take it away*!
Sarah (*saluting smartly*) I'll put it in the dustbin.

Sarah removes the mop and endeavours to hie Idle Jack on to her shoulder

Captain No, not *him*! THE MOP!

Sarah collects both the mop and the bucket and places them off-stage

(*on a very high, sustained note*) SQUAD!

Sarah returns

She hears the long note and runs in all directions to trace its origins. There is a pause

(*on an even higher note*) SQUAD!

Sarah runs this way and that hurriedly inspecting all the crew in her travels

SQUAD!

Sarah bumps into the Captain. She places her hands on her hips in happy relief

Sarah Oh, it's you!
Captain Of course it's me. Who the devil did you think it was?
Sarah I thought it was the foghorn.
Captain Get into line you stupid old scrubber. Company—Right turn!

They all do a smart right turn except Sarah, who turns left. She finds herself staring into the eyes of the Mate

Sarah (*to the Captain*) There's a man looking at me sir.

Act II, Scene 1   29

Captain (*bellowing*) Company—Face *front*!

They all face front except Sarah, who turns up-stage so that she has her back to the audience

Hi you! You!
Sarah (*giving the Mate a dig with her elbow*) Hi Mate, he's talking to you mate.
Captain Not him—you! Don't you know where your front is?
Sarah Yes sir. (*She gropes down her bosom and pulls out a large padded bra. She minces over to the Captain and dangles it in front of his face*) Here you are, sexy!
Captain (*beside himself*) *I* don't want it!
Sarah Well give it to lover-boy. (*She drapes the bra over the Mate's head*) He can use it for ear muffs.
Captain Company! Attention! Right turn—left turn—right turn—left turn—right turn—right turn—bout turn.
Sarah (*who has been going giddy*) Excuse me! I wish you'd make up your mind what you *do* want!

SONG (reprise)

There is a reprise of the previous naval number which they all sing as they march around the stage and off

The orchestra seques to a few bars of "The Sailors Hornpipe" and Mouser enters wearing a little sailor's hat and carrying a fish in his mouth. He dances round the stage doing the hornpipe very happily. If an accomplished dancer a full routine can be introduced

At the end of the dance Dick enters. He stares at Mouser in disbelief

Dick Mouser! You're aboard! You *did* follow me!

Mouser rolls over on his back kicking his legs in the air. Dick kneels and caresses him fervently

But how did you smuggle yourself aboard?

Mouser rises and mimes the dodging of the guard as he ran up the gangplank

I see! While the Mate's head was turned away . . . you bent right down . . . and then . . . you ran like the wind up the gangplank . . . and went into hiding. Clever boy!

Alice enters

Alice Dick!
Dick Alice! So you are aboard too.
Alice Shhh! I'm a stowaway.
Dick Your father's aboard too.
Alice I know. He's looking for *me*.
Dick The Captain's making him work his passage.
Alice Do him good, he needs a little exercise.

They both laugh, and Mouser holds his sides with glee as he lets forth a high-pitched giggle

I didn't know Mouser was here.

Dick I didn't know it myself till a few moments ago. Like you, he's a stowaway.

Alice Self-supporting by the look of it.

Mouser waggles the fish in the air and then offers it to Alice

Dick You forgot your bow.

Mouser drops the fish and makes a huge bow to Alice.

Alice replies with an outsize curtsy

Alice Dick, how wonderful, we're together again. You and I and Mouser.

SONG

If possible Mouser should be brought into this, possibly dancing between and around Dick and Alice during the singing. The duet can develop into a full-scale Production Number at the producer's discretion

Dick, Alice and Mouser exit at the end of the song

The Mate enters followed by Fitzwarren

Fitzwarren What's the matter Mate? You seem so annoyed.
Mate It's all these women aboard, that's what annoys me.
Fitzwarren I realize your way of life is no push-over.
Mate Push-over? You ought to be joking.
Fitzwarren It's been a salubrious experience to me. And a bit of an eye-opener.
Mate Eyeopener? Do you know what happened to me last night?
Fitzwarren No, do tell me.
Mate I retired to my cabin, innocent as a new-born lamb, and there, stretched right across my bunk was a lady's nightdress.
Fitzwarren Ah well, there's nothing in that.
Mate I know, that's what annoyed me.

Sarah enters

Sarah (*to Mate*) That washing machine in my cabin is no use at all, every time I put something in it it disappears.
Mate That's not a washing machine, that's the porthole.
Sarah What a pity, I've just put your spare pair of trousers in it.

Sarah exits

Mate Womin!

There is a rumble of thunder in the distance

Fitzwarren I say! The weather seems to be worsening. I don't like the way this ships rolling.

Act II, Scene 1   31

Mate Women always bring bad luck.
Fitzwarren Oh don't say that. I have reason to believe my daughter Alice is aboard.
Mate Oh, I don't mind her, she's a lovely little bit of ground bait.

There is another rumble of thunder, this time a little nearer

Fitzwarren (*giving a lurch*) Whoops! If you'll excuse me, I think I'll go below and lie down for a bit . . . I don't feel very well . . .

Fitzwarren exits hurredly

The Lights begin to dim

Idle Jack enters. A green lime picks him up

He rushes to the bulwark and leans over with his back to the audience, contorting his body in the manner of a seasick person

Mate (*jovially*) Lovely day!
Jack (*turning*) What's lovely about it?
Mate You need building up. What about a nice bit of pork with lots of crackling?
Jack Ooo! (*He rushes to the side again and leans over*)

There is another rumble of thunder

Sarah enters. A green lime picks her up

She dashes to the side of the ship and joins Jack, contorting her body even more so

Mate (*thoroughly enjoying himself*) What's for lunch cook?
Sarah (*turning and coming down a little*) Well, if we had some eggs you could have fried egg and bacon if we had some bacon.
Jack (*shouting*) Shut up talking about greasy bacon!
Mate For myself, I prefer a bit of salty ham with a lot of juicy fat.

Sarah and Idle Jack rush back to the bulwarks

Sarah (*over her shoulder*) I shall report *you* to the captain.
Mate Why bring him up.
Sarah I didn't know I'd swallowed him.
Jack (*coming down-stage*) Where's this old tub bound for?
Mate Barbary.
Sarah (*coming down-stage*) Where's Barbary?
Mate In Morocco. But I doubt if we'll make it. This weather! I have forebodings!
Sarah You're lucky. I've only got two—and they keep slipping. (*She adjusts her bust*)

There is a further roll of thunder, this time very loud

Mate I believe Old Father Neptune has put a curse on this ship.
Jack Father Who?
Mate Neptune. You know, the chap who rules the ocean. He's the king at the bottom of the sea.

Jack Ah well, so long as he stays down there.
Mate That's the trouble. If he doesn't like the look of you, he nips over the side of the ship, grabs you by the throat and, shiver me timbers, over you go! Down, down, to the bottom of the mighty ocean.
Sarah (*trembling violently*) Well, shiver me saucepan-lids, I hope he likes the look of me.
Mate Not if he's got any taste he wouldn't.
Jack I'm very fond of fish, I reckon he'd like me.

There is an enormous roll of thunder

Sarah Good job you're fond of fish—you've had your chips!

Father Neptune pops his head up from the other side of the bulwarks. He makes a dramatic gesture with his hands, then quickly disappears

(*addressing the audience*) What happened?... Did he?... Where?...
Mate Will you let us know if you see him?

Father Neptune appears from behind the bulwarks again. He disappears before the others can turn round

They race up-stage and look over the bulwarks in all directions

Father Neptune enters stage L whilst they have their backs turned, saunters to stage R and exits

The others then turn and run down stage. They address the audience

Sarah No, he's not there.
Mate I don't believe you saw him at all.
Jack You're pulling our legs.

Neptune enters from R and hovers

In response to audience advice the three comedians tiptoe towards the R exit and come face to face with Neptune. They turn and run towards the L exit

King Rat enters L

The comedians back away taking large, simultaneous steps. Neptune and Rat close in on them

Sarah, Mate and Jack exit in different directions

Neptune and Rat are left facing each other

Neptune	How nice to have you on the ship my friend, However doth this come to be?
Rat	I got fed up with the rat-race in Town And decided to go to sea.
Neptune	Are your minions in Barb'ry expecting you? Tell me, you scurvy old frisker,
Rat	Yes, I sent all the rats at the Palace so fair A message by telly-whisker.

Act II, Scene 2   33

Neptune   Well, I hope you've enjoyed your trip on this ship
                 'Cos I'm just about to sink her,
                 People call me the Old Man of the Sea,
                 In truth I'm a bit of a stinker.
Rat   Oh heavens! Don't sink her just yet Neppy boy,
                 For I've never learned to swim.
Neptune   Well, now's a good moment to start old dear,
                 Be my guest—Dive right in!

There is a mighty roll of thunder and a flash of lightning. Lights dim to deep blue

King Rat exits hastily

                 All creatures on this earth that creep,
                 Come, join the monsters of the deep,
                 Let mighty storm and tempest rip,
                 And sink this frail ill-fated ship!

Choristers and dancers enter from both sides. They race across stage screaming and shouting, exiting the opposite side and returning again and again till the end of the scene

Any storm effects should be introduced and the orchestra can play "storm music" at double-forte. Above the din can be heard the Captain's voice

Captain Take to the boats! Every man for himself!

Lights fade to complete Black-out

CURTAIN

SCENE 2

The Cruel Sea

The scene opens on No. 2 tabs. The storm music and effects continue, the lighting is deep blue and green

King Rat enters. He is apparently swimming, using his arms breast-stroke fashion. A Red Lime follows him. He faces front when half-way, the music drops to a whisper as he speaks. During his dialogue he adopts the attitude of a swimmer "treading water"

Rat   I soon learnt to swim,
                 'Twasn't easy by heck!
                 Guess I'm the only one
                 Saved from the wreck.

He turns and continues the swimming stroke, moving slowly till off-stage

The music rises to a crescendo and fades as we hear voices from the opposite side

Captain, Mate, Idle Jack and Fitzwarren enter. They are in a life boat, each one is pulling on an oar. (For details see Production Notes.) They walk backwards, with bent knees, moving slowly and giving the impression of rowing

All (*singing lustily*)
      A life on the ocean wave
      Is the only life for us,
      We've lost our blooming ship,
      Oh dash, and bother, and cuss!

They continue to sing till centre-stage, the movement then stops as they relax

Captain We're the only ones saved from the wreck. Any sign of land?
Mate (*rising and shading his eyes*) Not yet.
Captain Keep rowing.
Fitzwarren Half a tick skipper. My hands are blistered, can't we have a break?
Captain Pass him the Kit Kat.
Mate Don't talk of vittles at a time like this, I'm starving.
Fitzwarren I wonder if they've got any dry fish down there.

They all look over the side of the boat

Jack It'll be a bit wet if they have.
Mate Oh, there's a fish—look!
Jack Oooh! Poor fish, it's panting.
Mate So it is. Happy New Year fish!
Captain Why don't you drop it a line?
Fitzwarren Yes, that'd cure him.
Jack I've got an aunty who looks like that.
Captain I can quite believe it.
Jack (*letting forth a scream*) Oh! Look!
Others What's the matter?
Jack A sea-monster!
Others Where?
Jack Down there. It was glaring up at me. Look, there it is again.
Mate Fool! That's your own reflection. (*He leans towards Jack and points downwards*) See that?
Jack Yes, what is it?
Mate That's *my* face.
Jack Thank heavens, I thought it was mine.
Fitzwarren What a terrible storm last night.
Jack Was there a storm?
Fitzwarren Of course there was a storm, that's why our ship was sunk.
Jack Why didn't somebody wake me up, you *know* I can't sleep in a storm.
Mate It was raining cats and dogs.
Jack Raining cats and dogs? Is that worse than hailing taxis? (*He laughs heartily at his own joke*)
Captain Don't laugh like that, you're rocking the boat.
Mate (*rising suddenly*) Hey! What's that?
Captain What's what?

Act II, Scene 2   35

Mate (*excitedly pointing aft*) That ugly great thing following us!
Fitz It's a sea-monster.
Captain A sea-monster?
Fitzwarren Yes, a huge one. It's coming after us! Help!
Captain Quick lads. Pull for the shore! Pull hard!

They exit singing "A Life On The Ocean Wave"

Sarah enters as a mermaid

She floats across the stage, using her arms alternately breast-stroke and side-stroke. A pink lime follows her

Sarah I'm a mermaid that never murmurs! (*She looks off-stage*) Oh, there he is again! I'm being followed girls. Help! He's after me! He's after my barnacles. (*She hastens to the other side of the stage*)

Neptune enters

Neptune (*dramatically*) Ah, there you are! My little deep-sea mammal.
Sarah (*aside*) Father Christmas with a touch of gangrene!
Neptune Fear not, I am the Old Man of the Sea.
Sarah Thank heavens! I thought you were Jack the Kipper.
Neptune You were blown to me by the buffet!
Sarah Yes, I came in on a current.
Neptune You look so beautiful.
Sarah I feel like a fish out of water.
Neptune And yet, somehow you are not right for the ocean bed.
Sarah I'm all right for anybody's bed.
Neptune You are fashioned differently to other maids.
Sarah You can say that again.
Neptune You have legs!
Sarah Yes, and I've got water on my knee-caps.
Neptune But I *love* you.
Sarah You've got water on the brain.
Neptune The thrill, as you swish your flipping tail!
Sarah Take your flipping hands off. Fish fingers!

Neptune makes a pass at Sarah. She dodges him

Neptune Let us drift for ever on the same tide.
Sarah Don't like Tide, let's wash whiter with the Serf.
Neptune We will float upstream and I will show you my seaweed.
Sarah You dirty old dog-fish!
Neptune Be my little fish-wife, and share my oyster sea-shell.
Sarah Where do you live?
Neptune Two Filleted Place.

DUET

To the melody of "The Blue Danube", by Strauss. The first three movements only are used

1st *movement*

Neptune	A pretty young fish,
Sarah	Pish-pish! Pish-pish!
Neptune	Come give me a kiss,
Sarah	Pish-pish! Pish-pish!
Neptune	You dainty young dish,
Sarah	Pish-pish! Pish-pish!
Neptune	Of salty young miss,
Sarah	Pish-pish! Pish-pish!
	Please cover your gills,
Neptune	Flip-flip! Flop-flop!
Sarah	And stop getting thrills,
Neptune	Flop-flop! Flip-flip!
Sarah	I find it quite hard, to control,
	My new meta-morph-o-sis!

2nd *movement*

Neptune: Oh, I love you my—
Little tiddler,

Sarah: I have *never*—
Been a tiddler.

Neptune: I will marry you—
If you feel like it,

Sarah: I have never felt
So little like it—in my life.

3rd *movement*

Neptune: Come, swim along with me,
I'm as bouyant as can be, for
A bit of what you fancy
I'll give you a winkle
For your tea.

3rd *movement repeat*

Sarah: As sure as we are floating,
You surely must be joking,
I wish to tell you something,
A winkle's no use
Without a pin.

1st *movement repeat*

Neptune	Come, nibble my bait,
Sarah	You dinky thing,
Neptune	It's here, on a plate,
Sarah	You kinky thing,
Neptune	A juicy great worm,
Sarah	You slinky thing,
Neptune	A worm that won't turn,
Sarah	You stinky thing.
	Stop mucking about,
Neptune	Woof-woof! Waff-waff!
Sarah	You silly old trout,

Act II, Scene 4

Neptune	Waff-waff! Woof-woof!
Sarah	Your rod, I'm afraid,
	Is so crook'd,
	And I never will be hook'd

They repeat the last three lines in unison with ralluntando finish, Neptune changing words to first person

They exit after the song

Lights fade to Black-out

SCENE 3

Tabs open about half-way during Black-out disclosing small inset scene. Dick and the Cat are on a raft, pole in the centre to which Dick is clinging, the cat is squatting. The storm effects plus orchestra and any movement of raft which can be arranged is in full evidence

After a few seconds to enable the scene to be established, the effects die down as Fairy appears on stage R

Fairy Be of stout heart Dick. The journey may be long and arduous, but I have flung over you a net of magic. So be not afraid of the perils you may meet.

Dick I am humble with gratitude O Fairy. But what has happened to Alice, Alice my beloved?

Fairy	Alice is safe, I've seen to that,
	My concern now
	Is for you and your cat.
	Whilst wind and weather serve you,
	Cling to your frail craft,
	Let naught unnerve you,
	Your fight with evil
	Is all but won,
	May good luck speed you,
	'Til justice be done.

Fairy exits

SONG

Lights fade to Black-out

SCENE 4

Sultan's Palace of Barbary

A scene with a distinct Arabian flavour. A small dais runs at right-angles on which the Sultan sits watching the entertainers. He could be fanned by a slave

PRODUCTION NUMBER (Chorus)

If the Chorus is in Eastern dress the number can be applicable. If still in their previous costume they presumably are entertaining the Sultan with a song as prisoners

The Chorus exits

The Dancers enter

EASTERN DANCE (Dancers)

At the end of the dance the Dancers prostrate themselves before the Sultan. He claps his hands

The Dancers exit

A Sentinel enters

Sentinel (*salaaming*) More survivors from the wreck, O Mighty One.
Sultan Bring! (*He rises*)

Dick and Alice enter

Sultan Come hither! Closer! Tell me infidels, how come you to be here? Are you spies?
Dick No Sultan, we are not spies. We come as friends.
Alice We were on our way to you with precious merchandise, when we were shipwrecked.
Sultan You are in grave danger here. My Palace is over-run with rats. The whole Kasbah is besieged by these dangerous rodents.
Dick (*excitedly*) Sire! Maybe we can help.
Sultan You? How can you help?
Dick We have something that will destroy them.
Sultan (*doubtfully*) What *is* this "something"?
Dick A cat.
Sultan A what?
Dick An animal called a cat.
Sultan I know of no such animal.
Dick Wait here and we'll bring it to you.
Sultan If you speak the truth—then by Allah half my fortune shall be yours.
Dick We'll be right back.
Sultan (*to Sentinel*) Let them go.

Dick and Alice exit

Sultan (*resuming his seat on the rostrum*) I wonder, I wonder! (*He addresses the Sentinel*) Where are the new dancing girls I hear you speak of?
Sentinal They await without, O mighty Sultan.
Sultan Without what?
Sentinel Just . . . without.
Sultan What ere they are without, bring them within.

The Sentinel exits

Act II, Scene 4

The music strikes up and the Sultan settles down to enjoy the new spectacle

Sarah, Idle Jack, Captain and Mate enter

They are scantilly dressed in female attire of doubtful Eastern origin. They whirl round the stage in an ecstasy of delight as they belt out the words of the song

SONG: OH! SULTAN OF BARB'RY

Sarah Jack Captain Mate	} together	He is the boss of Barb'ry, and We like him very much, we Know some things about him, but We wouldn't mention such. He Wants us to perform for him, he's Got a dirty look, we'll Dance for him "Solomé", then We'll sling our blooming hook.

Chorus
Oh! Sultan of Barb'ry,
What a fine ruler you are.
Oh! Sultan of Barb'ry,
Tral-lal-lal-lal-lal-lal la.

Mate This silly sultry Sultan, who's
The boss of Barbary,

Captain Took quite a fancy to us, and
Invited us to tea.

Jack We'll have it in my chamber, said
The Sultan, silly clot.

Sarah We couldn't find his chamber, so
The plot has gone to pot.

Chorus
All Oh! Sultan of Barb'ry,
What a fine ruler you be,
Oh! Sultan of Barb'ry,
Riddle-ee riddle-ee ree.

Mate He's very hot on discipline, he
Likes to use the stick,

Captain It's stick for me, and stick for him, and
Stick for uncle Dick.

Jack He has a birthday very soon, with
Presents I suppose.

Sarah Well here's a pinch of snuff from me, to
Stick right up his nose.

Chorus
All Oh! Sultan of Barb'ry,
What a fine ruler are you,
Oh! Sultan of Barb'ry,

All
Fiddle and Faddle and Pooh!
Well, that's our singing finished, and we've
Done our very best, so
Now we'll do our laundry, and get
Changed our dirty vest, and
When we've washed our finery, we'll
Hang it up on pegs, but
First of all we'll do our dance, and
Shake our hairy legs.

They now go into a burlesque Eastern Dance. The dance can be quite simple so long as it contains eccentric Eastern hand movements

They finish the dance and stand in a row. The Sultan comes down-stage and stands to one side. He speaks in a slow deliberate voice

Sultan Come hither the ugly one!

They look at each other, and Sarah gives Jack a nudge

Sarah Go on, he means you.
Jack No, he means you, you're uglier than what I am.
Captain I reckon he means the Mate, he's the ugliest sailor *I've* ever seen.
Mate I'll toss you for it.
Jack No, I've got a better idea. (*He points as he speaks*) Eeny-meeny-miney-mo, before the Sultan you must go! It's you Sarah.
Sarah You didn't include yourself, that's not fair.
Sultan (*bellowing*) The ugliest one of all—*come forth*!

There is a short pause whilst they form a ring and observe each other at close quarters. They then straighten up the line and walk forward in unison. The Sultan glares at them for a moment and then points to Sarah, shouting at the top of his voice

You!

The others scamper to the opposite side and cling together for protection

Sarah There's no need to shriek, Sheik.
Sultan Silence! You're too ugly for the Harem, I'll have you beheaded instead.
Sarah (*over her shoulder, to the others*) Makes a nice change, doesn't it.
Sultan Silence, faggot!
Sarah Before you chop my head off will you grant me one request.
Sultan Well?
Sarah Can I have a walk round the block?
Sultan (*beside himself with temper*) I feel quite faint.
Sarah (*sympathetically*) Ooh! Perhaps it's something you've eaten.
Sultan It is *not* something I've eaten. It's . . .
Sarah It's flown to your stomach and made you feel a bit umfidoodle-em.
Sultan (*shouting himself hoarse*) I am NOT feeling umfidoodle-em!
Sarah Well, a bit hangdoggy then.

Act II, Scene 4

Sultan I am NOT a . . . Take them to the dungeons!

The Stage lights suddenly dim, there is a bright flash and a loud noise like a heavy roll of thunder

   King Rat enters

Sarah screams and joins the others

Sultan Who are you?
Rat I am King Rat!
Sultan What do you want?
Rat Your kingdom—your throne!
Sultan (*backing away in despair*) Spare me! Spare me!
Rat My rats are everywhere. Your palace is beseiged. As I live they will conquer and destroy you.
Sultan No! No!
Rat (*advancing on him*) Yes! Yes! And you shall be the last to go. I will eat you alive!
Sultan Help! Help!
Rat There is no one who can help you.

   Dick, Alice and Fitzwarren enter

Dick Oh yes there is!

   Mouser bounces on

Dick After him, Mouser!

Fight music begins

The Rat shrinks back but quickly recovers himself. Mouser faces up to him The Rat makes a grab, Mouser side-steps. They spar again. Mouser grabs the Rat's leg, they both roll on the floor. They roll over and over each other. The rest of the fight can be at the producer's discretion. Ultimately the Rat, who appears to be getting the best of it, makes a determined stance with legs wide apart. Mouser seizes his opportunity and darts between his legs. He forthwith jumps on his back, and gradually the Rat sinks to the floor. Mouser rises and stands over the Rat placing his foot on his chest. Everyone cheers

Sultan Well done! To whom does this . . . er . . . cat belong.
Dick He is mine.
Sultan And who are you?
Dick My name is Dick Whittington. This is Alderman Fitzwarren and his daughter Alice.
Alice (*bowing gracefully*) How do you do.
Fitzwarren Charmed I'm sure.
Sultan And the cat?
Dick His name is Mouser. Mouser! Take a bow.

Mouser leaves the Rat and goes forward with a large bow which the Sultan acknowledges. The Rat suddenly leaps to his feet and makes to attack Mouser. But the cat overpowers him again

All Kill it! Kill it!

The Fairy enters

Fairy Nay! Spare him!
Alice A Fairy!
Dick It's *my* Fairy! The one I once told you about, remember?

They stand looking at the Fairy in disbelief

Jack I'm completely confusticated!
Captain I'm dumfounded!
Sarah I'm decarbonized!
Fairy Once the Rat is killed all the others will die too. But first—King Rat has something to say. Go on, King Rat.
Rat (*now on his knees*) Your magic is too great for me. What can I say?
Fairy A confession I think, to the Alderman.
Fitzwarren (*coming forward*) Well?
Rat T'was I who stole the necklace from the safe and put it in Dick's bundle.
Fitzwarren You? (*To Dick*) How can you ever forgive me?
Alice Oh Dick, I knew it would all come right in the end.
Fairy   And now Rat, your end is nigh,
                 I want all rats to see you die,
                 Then no more wrong do I envisage.
Rat   Hold on, Fairy Sugar-Plum!
                 You're killing my public image!
Fairy   Your just deserts you've surely got,
                 I hope in hell to see you rot.
Rat   Okay, I cannot fight such principles as yours are,

(*He leans across the footlights and addresses the audience*)

                 Fancy me! A rotting rat!
                 How terribly, terribly bourgeois!

He crawls off on his knees

The Fairy exits

Sultan Your gallantry overwhelms me.
Dick Don't thank me. It's all thanks to Mouser.
Sultan Nevertheless, I will keep my promise. Half my fortune shall be yours.
All Hooray!
Sultan And I will arrange for a ship to take you all back to England.
Jack What about us, Mister Sultana?
Sultan I was only joking. Of course you are released.

Sarah, Jack, Captain and Mate cheer heartily

   All except . . . this one!
Sarah Me?
Sultan Yes! You!

Act II, Scene 5

Sarah puts on a pathetic look and makes a motion across her throat with her finger

No, not the cold chop! I've decided to make you the head girl in my Harem.

The Sultan gives Sarah a playful dig in the ribs

Sarah Oh, don't be so cheeky Sheiky!

PRODUCTION NUMBER

This should be something applicable to the situation and preferably a number in which the Choristers and Dancers participate

At the end of the song the Lights fade to Black-out

Scene 5

King Rat enters, still crawling on his knees. He is followed by The Fairy

Fairy King Rat, You've had your dirty day, you know,
 The proof is quite abundant,
Rat Oh yes, I used to be a rodent once,
 Alas! Now I'm redundant.
Fairy You'll have to be forgiven,
 'Cos that's usual I suppose.
Rat Yes, well hurry up. It's cold down here,
 My feet are getting froze.
Fairy Froze? My feet are getting froze?
 That's a terrible rhyme. E'en for pantomime,
 I'm surprised that you saw fit to use it.
Rat It's a habit of mine, when making a rhyme,
 To muck it about and abuse it.
Fairy Don't be such a dunce. Go home at once,
 And try harder with your good appliance.
Rat Right, I'll crawl down me hole. Sign on for the dole,
 And donate my body to science.
Fairy It's time you were dead. So please go to bed,
 I wish you goodbye. And good night!
Rat Okay! When I'm gone. You can sing 'em a song,
 That'll serve the lot of 'em right.

King Rat crawls off

SONG

She exits after her song

Sarah and Idle Jack enter

Sarah does her MEE-OW gag with the audience

Sarah (*to Jack*) Isn't it wonderful news about Dick Whittington? He's going to be made Lord Mayor of London.

Jack No!
Sarah Yes! (*Thoughtfully*) I wonder if he wants a good cook?
Jack (*dreamily*) I wonder if he wants a valet to sleep in?
Sarah You could do the sleeping part all right.
Jack But I thought you were going to be made head girl in the harem?
Sarah Yes, that pagan potentate thought I was up for grabs.
Jack Aren't you then?
Sarah Oh no! I told him my fairy godmother wouldn't allow it.
Jack You haven't got a fairy godmother.
Sarah No, but I've got a sissy uncle.
Jack I'm so happy for Dicky Whit, I feel I want to sing.
Sarah So do I. Here, tell you what, let us *all* sing. (*To audience*) Will you sing with us? . . . Right!

COMMUNITY CHORUS SONG

This is the usual popular chorus song in which the audience join in, possibly with a song-sheet, and maybe children invited on to the stage

SCENE 6

The Guildhall London

An elaborate scene with a courtly atmosphere. A high rostrum runs across the back with an embellised staircase leading down from the centre. As much pomp and circumstance as possible should accompany the scene

When the Curtain rises the ceremony is already under way. The dignitaries (choristers) are all assembled, Dick is centre stage, on either side stands the Cryer and the Lord Chamberlain. Sword-bearer and late Lord Mayor are also close by

OLD TIME MADRIGAL

Sung by all on stage with feeling and harmony

At the end of the singing the Cryer speaks

Cryer O Yes! O Yes! O Yes! I hereby announce; you good men of the livery have been summoned to appear here this day to attend the installation of the new Lord Mayor of London.
Sword-bearer I herewith place this chain of office upon the Lord Mayor elect. (*He places the chain round Dick's neck*)
Lord Chamberlain I present you with the City Sceptre. (*He does so*).
Cryer I present you with the Mace. (*He does so*).
Late Mayor And I present you with the Key of the City. (*He does so*).
Cryer I further asseverate that you, Dick Whittington, have been chosen as a fit and able person to be Lord Mayor of the City of London for the ensuing year.
Dick I beg to thank the court for the honour thus conferred on me.

All on stage cheer

  Alice and Fitzwarren enter

Act II, Scene 6

Alice Oh Dick, I'm so proud of you.
Fitzwarren (*offering his hand*) Congratulations me boy! And my humblest apologies. What can I ever do to make amends for the awful wrong I did you?
Dick Simple! Give me your daughter's hand in marriage.
Fitzwarren That I do wholeheartedly. But does the lady agree?
Alice Oh Dick! (*She embraces him*) You once said you didn't believe the streets of London were paved with gold.
Dick They are—if you find the right girl. We'll get married right away, if you'll have me.
Alice (*laughingly*) Right away!
Fitzwarren Dick! Do you realize, you are now one of *us*. A real Londoner!
Dick Yes, isn't it wonderful. London Town, the place I've always loved so much.

PRODUCTION NUMBER

(*Song suggested; "Maybe It's Because I'm A Londoner" By Hubert Gregg. Published by E.M.I.—Frances, Day, and Hunter*)

Dick commences the number, all on stage join in

The Dancers enter and do a suitable routine

All exit after the number except Fitzwarren

Sarah, Idle Jack, Captain and Mate enter

Sarah Isn't it all exciting! Let's do something to celebrate. Play a game or something.
Fitzwarren Let's play that game *Give Us A Clue*.
Sarah Oh yes! But first I have something to say. (*She does her MEE-OW gag with the audience*) How do you play this game?
Fitzwarren There's several ways you can do it.
Captain I've played it many times when aboard. Somebody makes a sign, or does a gesture, and the others have to guess what it is he's doing.
Fitzwarren Splendid! Go on Captain, you start.

The Captain dodges about waving his right arm as though striking something

Captain Go on, what am I doing, what am I doing? (*He keeps the movement going*)

The others shout suggestions

All (*not in unison*) Waving goodbye! Knocking a nail in! Going crazy! Smashing up the telly! Knocking snow off the car!
Captain (*stopping the movement*) No! Do you give it up?
All Yes. What were you doing?
Captain Playing tennis! (*He repeats the movement to prove his point*)
All Ooh!
Jack It's exciting. May I have a go?
All Yes.

Jack (*jumping about and waving his right arm in exactly the same manner as the Captain*) Go on, what am I doing, what am I doing?
Fitzwarren That's ridiculous! You're doing the same as the Captain did, playing tennis.
Jack No, catching butterflies!
All Oooh! (*In derision*) Catching butterflies!
Sarah I've got one! (*She runs hither and thither with her feet splayed out, zigzagging and whirling in all directions*) Go on what am I doing, what am I doing?
All (*not in unison*) Playing football! Dancing the Polka! Chasing a man! Knees up Mother Brown!
Sarah (*stopping the movement*) Give it up?
Fitzwarren Yes, what are you doing?
Sarah Ice skating!
Jack (*disgustedly*) Ice skating? She didn't fall down once!
Sarah No, I'm a very good skater, I was practically brought up on skates.
Jack I always thought there was something a bit fishy about you.
Fitzwarren Now, tell you what. I'll do one, and from now on let the audience join in. (*To the audience*) Will you? Okay then. Off we go! (*Fitzwarren opens wide his two hands then brings them sharply together, repeating the movement ad lib*) Go on, what am I doing?
Captain (*after audience reaction*) That's a difficult one Fitzy, no one can guess it. What were you doing?
Fitzwarren (*repeating the movement*) Measuring cloth!
All Ooh!
Sarah (*dashing to centre-stage*) I've thought of one. (*To the audience*) What am I doing? (*She half-sits and uses her two hands alternately up and down as though yanking at something in the air*) Go on! What am I doing, what am I doing?
Fitzwarren (*when audience reaction has gone far enough*) Okay, okay! I don't think anybody got it right. What *were* you doing Sarah?
Sarah Milking a cow. (*She repeats the movement to prove her point*)
Jack Oh, I've thought of a beauty. You'll never guess it. (*He takes exactly the same attitude as Sarah and uses his two hands in the same way*) Go on! What am I doing?
Fitzwarren Once again you're being stupid. We *all* know what you're doing. You're milking a cow.
Jack No, ringing church bells.
All (*in disgust*) Ooh!
Mate I haven't done one yet.
Captain Well, nobody's stopping you. Do something.

The Mate settles himself centre-stage, stands smartly to attention and then relaxes, making no movement at all

Mate Go on, what am I doing?
Captain Well do something.
Mate I'm doing it.
Captain Do your charade.

Act II, Scene 6

Mate I am.
Captain You're not.
Mate I am.
Captain Shiver me timbers, what are you doing?
Mate I'm going upstairs.
All (*incredulously*) Going upstairs?
Captain But you're standing perfectly still.
Mate That's right. I'm in a lift.
Captain (*annoyed*) Go on, do something else.

The Mate stands perfectly still as before

Mate Okay, off we go.
Captain Well, start.
Mate I have.
Captain You haven't.
Mate I have. (*He appeals to the audience*) What am I doing?
Captain (*after audience reaction*) We all know what you're doing, the same as last time. Going upstairs in a lift.
Mate No! Coming down this time.
Captain Look here, do something else, something we can all understand. And stop going up and down in a lift.
Mate Aye, aye Capt'n. I'll give you an easy one. You ought to get this one Captain, this is something I do every time I'm ashore. (*He does a little running movement*) I'm coming down the gangplank now, I'll give you that bit for nothing. (*He does a sailors-roll walk in a figure-eight round the stage. Then knocks on an imaginary door. The door presumably being opened he throws his arms around an imaginary person who he kisses violently again and again*) Go on, what am I doing, what am I doing?
Captain (*when audience reaction has gone far enough*) I know what you're doing. You're kissing your wife!
Mate No! Kissing yours!

General reaction as the introductory music strikes up for the next number

SONG

A jolly number, preferably something with a modern flavour

They all exit after the song

The Dancers enter and perform a Cat Ballet (or any dance speciality)

The Dancers exit after the ballet

A Flunkey enters up-stage. He walks across the rostrum and remains standing at the top of the staircase as he announces the March Down

The cast march along the rostrum to suitable March Down music, and down the stairs for their "call" as their names are announced

Flunkey My Lords, Ladies and Gentlemen of the Chorus

The Choristers enter

The Guildhall Terpsichoreans.

The Dancers enter

His eminence the Sultan of Barbary.

Sultan enters

That Old Man of the sea—Father Neptune.

Neptune enters

Fairy Sugar Plum and King Rat.

Fairy and King Rat enter

Mouser the Cat.

Mouser enters

His loftiness—Alderman Fitzwarren.

Fitzwarren enters

His lowliness—Idle Jack.

Idle Jack enters

Captain Fairweather and his Mate.

Captain and Mate enter

That humble, humdrum old humbug—Sarah the cook.

Sarah enters. She walks to the footlights and does her MEE-OW gag with the audience

The music now seques immediately to a few bars of "The Wedding March" as the Flunkey makes the next announcement

The Lord Mayor of London and his lady wife Alice.

Dick and Alice enter followed by the Children who are dressed as pages and bridesmaids (optional)

The music now stops as the Fairy steps forward and speaks

Fairy Present to me my magic sword.

A Chorister hands the sword to the Fairy. The Fairy then motions Dick to kneel, which he does. She forthwith touches him lightly on either shoulder with the tip of the sword

With this bright blade I confer upon you a knighthood. (*Very deliberately*) Arise! Sir Richard Whittington, Lord Mayor of London.

All on stage cheer. The music strikes up for the finale

FINALE CHORUS

This can be a reprise of one of the popular numbers previously sung in the production

CURTAIN

FURNITURE AND PROPERTY LIST

ACT 1
Scene 1

On stage: Milestone, with "London 5 miles" on it
General dressing of flowers, trees etc
Off stage: Picnic hampers. Contents include cups, cake, pies, tea, coffee, wine bottle, sausages, potato chips, "souffle" **(Dancers)**
Personal: **Dick:** bundles and stick
Jack: fly swat, photograph
Alice: necklace, bill, camera
Mate: ditty bag
Fitzwarren: pound note, dog biscuit

Scene 2
No properties required

Scene 3
On stage: Two counters
Safe
General dressing for store including packet of nappies by Sarah's counter
Chair
Off stage: Kitbag **(Jack)**
Paper parcels **(Sarah)**
Hat, coat, case **(Alice)**
Personal: **1st Man:** bag of moth balls
4th Lady: pencil, paper
3rd Man: mask, gun
Fitzwarren: two keys
Alice: necklace (from scene 1)
Dick: bundle and stick
Mouser: property mouse

ACT 2
Scene 1

On stage: Upper deck of a ship, plus dressing as desired
Off stage: Mops on poles **(Chorus)**
Flags **(Chorus)**
Bucket and mop **(Sarah)**
Large box **(Jack)**
Personal: **Sarah:** padded bra
Mouser: sailor hat, fish

Scene 2
Off stage: Boat **(Captain, Mate, Jack, Fitzwarren)**

SCENE 3

Off stage: Raft **(Dick and Cat)**

SCENE 4

No properties required

SCENE 5

No properties required

SCENE 6

Off stage: Sword **(Chorister)**
  Chain of office **(Sword-bearer)**
  Sceptre **(Lord Chamberlain)**
  Mace **(Cryer)**

LIGHTING PLOT

Property fittings required: nil
Various simple settings

ACT 1, SCENE 1

To open	Bright, exterior sunlight	
Cue 1	**Dick:** "I'm just down and out!"	(Page 2)
	Lights dim to spot on Fairy	
Cue 2	**Dick:** "How could I ever become . . ."	(Page 2)
	Lights up to full	
Cue 3	Souffle shatters	(Page 11)
	Black-out	

ACT 1, SCENE 2

To open Darkness

Cue 4	**King Rat** enters	(Page 11)
	Red spot on Rat	
Cue 5	**Fairy Sugar Plum** enters	(Page 12)
	White spot on Fairy	
Cue 6	**Dick and Mouser** enter	(Page 13)
	Lights up to full	
Cue 7	At end of song	(Page 14)
	Slow fade to Black-out	

ACT 1, SCENE 3

To open Bright, general lighting

Cue 8	**Dick, Sarah and Jack** exit after song	(Page 18)
	Lights dim, red spot on Rat	
Cue 9	As **King Rat** exits	(Page 19)
	Lights up to full	
Cue 10	As **King Rat** enters	(Page 22)
	Red spot on Rat	
Cue 11	As **King Rat** exits	(Page 22)
	Lights up to full	

ACT 2, SCENE 1

To open General lighting

Cue 12	**Fitzwarren** exits hurriedly	(Page 31)
	Lights dim	
Cue 13	**Jack** enters	(Page 31)
	Green spot picks Jack up	

Cue 14	**Sarah** enters *Green spot picks Sarah up*	(Page 31)
Cue 15	**Neptune:** ". . . —Dive right in." *Flash, lights dim to deep blue*	(Page 33)
Cue 16	**Captain:** "Every man for himself!" *Fade to Black-out*	(Page 33)

ACT 2, SCENE 2

To open Deep blue and green storm lighting

Cue 17	**King Rat** enters *Red spot on Rat*	(Page 33)
Cue 18	**King Rat** exits *Cut red spot*	(Page 33)
Cue 19	**Sarah** enters *Pink spot on Sarah*	(Page 35)
Cue 20	**Neptune** enters *Green follow spot on Neptune*	(Page 35)
Cue 21	**Neptune and Sarah** exit *Fade to Black-out*	(Page 37)

ACT 2, SCENE 3

To open Steel blue lime on half-stage

Cue 22	**Fairy** enters *Spot on fairy, fade on exit*	(Page 37)

ACT 2, SCENE 4

To open Interior lighting

Cue 23	**Sultan:** "Take them to the dungeons!" *Lights dim. Flash. Red spot on Rat*	(Page 41)
Cue 24	**Fairy** enters *Spot on Fairy until exit*	(Page 42)
Cue 25	At end of song *Fade to Black-out*	(Page 43)

ACT 2, SCENE 5

To open Dim Lighting

Cue 26	**King Rat and Fairy** enter *Red spot on Rat, white spot on Fairy*	(Page 43)
Cue 27	After **Fairy** exits *Lights up to full*	(Page 43)

ACT 2, SCENE 6

To open Bright general lighting
No cues

EFFECTS PLOT

ACT 1

Cue 1	**Fairy:** "Fame and fortune is awaiting you." *Bells ring*	(Page 2)
Cue 2	**Captain:** ". . . our half was at the bottom." *Buzzing bee*	(Page 10)
Cue 3	**Alice:** "Dead still everyone." *Buzzing bee*	(Page 11)
Cue 4	As **King Rat** enters *Magnesium flash*	(Page 18)

ACT 2

Cue 5	**Mate:** "Womin!" *Distant thunder*	(Page 30)
Cue 6	**Mate:** ". . . bit of ground bait." *Rumble of thunder*	(Page 31)
Cue 7	**Jack** rushes to side of ship (2nd time) *Thunder*	(Page 31)
Cue 8	**Sarah:** ". . . and they keep slipping." *Very loud thunder*	(Page 31)
Cue 9	**Jack:** ". . . reckon he'd like me." *Large roll of thunder*	(Page 32)
Cue 10	**Neptune:** ". . .—Dive right in!" *Roll of thunder*	(Page 33)
Cue 11	**Neptune:** ". . . frail, ill-fated ship." *Storm effects*	(Page 33)
Cue 12	At opening of Scene 2 *Storm effects continuous during scene*	(Page 33)
Cue 13	At opening of Scene 3 *Storm effects continue*	(Page 37)
Cue 14	**Sultan:** "Take them to the dungeons!" *Roll of thunder*	(Page 41)

TURN AGAIN WHITTINGTON — Arranged Verne Morgan

THE IRISH WASHERWOMAN — Arranged Verne Morgan

MADE AND PRINTED IN GREAT BRITAIN BY
LATIMER TREND & COMPANY LTD PLYMOUTH
MADE IN ENGLAND

www.ingramcontent.com/pod-product-compliance
Ingram Content Group UK Ltd.
Pitfield, Milton Keynes, MK11 3LW, UK
UKHW021847210426
53221PUK00022B/515